REVEALED IN THE PIT

Louis Lopez

REVEALED IN THE PIT
A PRISONERS JOURNAL
By
Louis Lopez

LOUIS LOPEZ

PUBLISHED by PARABLES
Earthly Stories with a Heavenly Meaning

REVEALED IN THE PIT
LOUIS LOPEZ

Published By Parables
September, 2018

All Rights Reserved. No part of this book may be reproduced or utilized in any form or by any means, electronic or mechanical, including photocopying, recording, or by any information storage and retrieval system, without permission in writing from the author.

    ISBN 978-1-945698-84-2
    Printed in the United States of America

REVEALED IN THE PIT

Readers should be aware that Internet Web sites offered as citations and/or sources for further information may have been changed or disappeared between the time this was written and the time it is read.

REVEALED IN THE PIT
A PRISONERS JOURNAL
By
Louis Lopez

LOUIS LOPEZ

Contact Information

P.O. BOX 392004
DENVER, CO 80239-8004
phone 720 320-1275
gbd.lal@outlook.com

About This Book – About The Author

This is the journal I kept while I was in solitary confinement, my thoughts and prayers in a place of desolation. I wanted people to read it because I feel like it will bring hope and strength in times when life seem impossible. If I can find hope and truth in one of the darkest places on Earth, I believe anyone can do the same in all life struggles.

The main idea of this journal is the changing and condition of the mind under duress. Also, I wanted you, the reader, to see how similar and human we all are. So, take a good look into my mind while in the darkness. Feel free to share my journal with those who can't find hope in their situation or lives.

Colossians 2.5 says, "For though I am absent in body, yet I am with you in spirit, rejoicing to see your good order and the firmness of your faith in Christ". Also, words from a man living in the darkness with chains and mine to you and anyone else who wants to listen. I pray all are blessed with this journal from the pit.

Louis Lopez

REVEALED IN THE PIT

Seg. December 13, 2016 – Tuesday

    Lord God of mercy and grace. My God of everlasting to everlasting. Unsearchable are your ways and your kingdom are without end. I come to your throne only by the name of your son Jesus. Please, Father, hear the prayer from your servant today. May the blood of Jesus cleanse me of all my sins. I have fallen short of the obedience of my faith Lord, I have looked to earthly things for comfort and haven't given you all my praise. My unthankful way has quieted your voice in my life. Please my God, forgive your son. I am in the pit of separation from all things now, and it's clear you love me in ways I am to fleshly to understand. Please forgive me Lord Jehovah. I am crushed, and my eyes are full of tears for my ways of disobedience. I know my choices lately are not what you teach. I only have authority through Jesus name to overcome and persevere all things. I truly want to please you Lord. Search me in all ways and rebuke the things that hinder my walk with you. I believe in you and I believe your son Jesus lived, suffered and resurrected for all the sins of the world. I am sick Lord, only because of my falling away from your light. Restore and redeem me Father. Forget my selfishness and release me from the guilt of my transgressions. I'm so sorry Father. I only struggle because I don't look to your rest. I am burdened only because I choose to carry it. I am weak and cannot bear them without you. Without you I am lost. You have given me so much even in this storm. You and only you deserve my thanks in prayer and worship. Thank you for your sacrifice that erases my sins. Lord Jesus please forgive me for all my ways and thoughts that don't glorify your name. Thank you for bringing me low in suffering. Thank you for your intervention in my life because I know I don't deserve the life and light you give the world. Father, my prayer is that you provide me strength to endure this labor. This imprisonment hurts me and our loved ones, and I need your peace for all. You are all things and, in all things, please help me to understand my suffering as it is your will. Help me to be humble and to look for only your hands for instruction and security. Reveal your love and forgiveness to all my children, my mom and all your children. As the Angels of Heaven remain with faithful watch over me, please Lord let them not take their eyes off the ones I love. Keep your hedge of protection around my family, especially through this time of imprisonment and separation. Lord Jesus I love you so much and I am so thankful that you loved me first. Hear my prayer today Lord. Only through the name above all names Jesus Christ can my prayers be brought to my Almighty God and Father. Heal us Lord in Jesus name, Amen.

Louis Lopez

REVEALED IN THE PIT

<u>Seg. December 15, 2016 – Thursday Morning</u>
God be merciful to me, a sinner…

As I sit in segregation my mind wonders to so many places. I've been sitting here completely alone with God. I've been placed in this situation by no wrong doing of my own. I am here because of association with the very people I try to help. Still, I feel guilty somehow.

I think I'm cursed or even a wicked man. I do so well and right by God most days, other days I allow my old selfish ways to lead me in the way of faithlessness. I will never stop believing in God or his son Jesus Christ. I know my faith is real. What I'm struggling with at this point in my life, is if I'm worthy of being saved.

Am I the wicked one the bible talks about? Am I the stumbling block Jesus speaks about in the bible? I am a very sensitive man. I love people who treat me like dirt. I love people who treat me like they love me. I also hurt these people. When will this end?

I walk around with a "knot" in my stomach at all times of my life, whether I'm here in a box (literally) or out with the ones I love. I always am hurting! I hate to complain! I don't want to be weak. I'm just sick of suffering. I hope God helps me soon. I am thinking about death more often now, than ever before. Sometimes, I don't see how it could harm me or anyone else more than my life already has.

The holidays are here, and they are precious to me. Today it's a possibility I spend my favorite time of year in a cage. Last year I was with all the people I love, last year we ate, sang and danced our way into the new year. How much can I take? How many more tears must I shed until God releases me from this painful life?

God has given me strength throughout my whole life. Strength to endure all things deserved and not deserved. Why is my price so high? I cannot continue living with such high prices on all aspects of my being. My heart is weak, and it causes my whole body to be weary. Today I will live because God commands it. But full of tears, I regretfully hope it's not His will I live for tomorrow…

REVEALED IN THE PIT

<u>Seg. December 15, 2016 – Thursday night</u>

Today through study, I realized more about why God wants me alive. This situation is His way of showing me His grace. I know I will be released from this soon. I know because I haven't done anything wrong. So, knowing that, I realized today, that this is for God.

Today He spoke to me and asked that I quiet my mind and let him fill my heart. He stopped my tears and actually had me laugh today as I re-read the story of Joseph. How he was sold and imprisoned. I was comforted by Joseph's faith and determination to love with faith <u>always.</u>

I really believe in the word of God. In this my weakness, I know that through it, then I am strong. I am fully prepared now, to let go of the things that are hindering my destiny. I am restored with ideas to reach out to others with the truth of Gods light.

This suffering is God's will for me tonight. So, no more complaining and more faith in all things for my Lord and Savior. So much was revealed to me today. I searched and searched to see if I was cursed. Funny thing is, I was born of the flesh, but I know re-born in the Spirit. I Will live! Amen

REVEALED IN THE PIT

<u>Seg. December 16, 2019 – Friday</u>

Today has been a tough one so far, I still haven't heard anything from anyone. I've been locked down for 72 hours straight. Thank God they gave me a bible and some stationary

I've been thinking a lot about my relationship. How we started, to how things are between us now. There were times I think we honestly felt there was no way we could ever be apart, other times we couldn't wait to get away from one another, In retrospect, no one has deliberately hurt me the way she has.

Today I remember the first time we kissed. I remember how many times I protected her. Unfortunately, it's also not hard to recall all the times I failed her too. Lately she's been terribly distant, I mean, she tells me she loves me, but for some reason she is unable to show me. I haven't seen her or our kids for eight months!

    She cries to me over the phone. She tells me everything about her life. I love that about her. She tells the truth, she is usually extremely honest with me. It makes me feel important to her. Today, I am still madly in love with all she is. I guess I can never see myself loving anyone else. I hope God keeps us together. I really want her to be my wife.

    We talk about God and I've never prayed with or for someone more than I have her. She has seized my heart. Even if I try to let her go, I cannot. Today, so far, is full of thoughts for my love, maybe she is thinking of me too. My prayers are dedicated to the woman I love today...

    Lord God, the Father and Creator of all, the great I am; from the throne of eternity I am humbled by Your Majesty. Today and always, I recognize the love that you are, and I thank you for the gift of grace. Your love overwhelms me, and it always becomes unsearchable as I get close to you. My heart is burdened, Lord please forgive me for the worry I sometimes carry. Your word is life and you, through your son Jesus Christ, give us perfect reason to live this life worry free. Help me to grasp your will and bind my life to it. I'm condemned by the world and set in a place for the outcast of this society. You and only you have the power to set men free, or to condemn. You are the one who loves and gives forgiveness through the suffering of your Son Jesus. Through His name, I ask for peace and love. I beg of you to hear my prayer during this dark season of my life. This prayer is not for self, but for the woman I love. She is your daughter and loves you in body and spirit. Help me Lord to understand your will as it pertains to our union. Even as we never deserved your gifts and grace, you blessed us with three children. Although two of the children are not of my seed; you with impossible power made it possible for them to be given over to my love and fatherhood. You made me their Dad! You are all things and in all things Lord God. So today I ask you to keep them protected, keep worry captive in mine and their mother's hearts. Help us to love one another the way Christ shows and teaches. By the power of the name Jesus Christ, give us authority to overcome this storm and separation. I raise my family up to you Father, to heal and bless as you will. Give us all strength to endure as you work in me, your son and saint. I believe only you can correct our shortcomings and dispel our past failures. Through the blood of Jesus Christ. I give all and my life over to you. I surrender Father. Amen

Louis Lopez

REVEALED IN THE PIT

Seg. December 16, 2016 – evening

Let me just say God is good! I realized today, through God, why I'm here (solitary confinement). I was thinking about death way too much. I was worrying myself with the negativity only Satan will bring. My thoughts and demeanor promoted death, and it was too close for God's purpose in my life.

I asked the Lord, "why?", and He said, "Son, this is just a precaution to ensure that you live". Right now, I'm overwhelmed by my Father, I am restored and have a strong hope in my situation and for what's to come. I am preparing my mind, through the Holy Spirit for the victory God has prepared for me. I have tons of scripture that truly are the breath of Gods voice in my life.

Through the prophet Isaiah (30:18) God let me know the security He offers me today, yesterday and in all times to come. I will wait patiently on my God. For anyone who might read these words, know the Great I Am, Elohim, Lord Jehovah is real and His sacrifice through Jesus is the only reason this prisoner lives and loves. Amen

Seg. December 17, 2016 – Saturday morning

So, this morning I woke up struggling with wrongful thoughts. I'm reading the word and praying. God is so great, and His grace is overwhelming! His words this morning brought me to tears.

He showed me that I need to stop the worrying and false thoughts I create in my mind. He explained that my disobedience starts with the thoughts. I choose every moment of every day. Put on the mind of Christ!! I keep letting the enemy put strongholds in my mind. All the things I think about that bring me despair, are a whole bunch of lies!!!

Renewing my mind and the thoughts thereof is imperative to moving toward the promises of my Father.

Today I'm practicing being positive and thinking good things about all that I am and have only through the graces of God. Gosh, I have something big ahead. I don't know what but it's best I start preparing before than during!! Today I will rest in the Lord and quiet my mind, so I can experience instruction from the Holy Spirit. His guidance is so imperative in all things! I long to hear Him. Hear my prayer through the Name of Jesus… Amen

Seg. December 17, 2016 – Saturday Night

Today was a productive but difficult one. It's my 6th day in solitary confinement. I've been one on one with my God today. He had me laugh and cry, I realize the error of my way these last few months. Although He pointed out the truth, He also always lets me know He loves me and encourages me to "live".

I have some great plans for the next year. I am shedding, through the Word, so much hindrance from my mind and spirit. Boy, has God got my attention. I am so glad I am saved without "knowing" I would never be able to "hear". God is using me and loving me all the time.

I don't know what He has in store for me tomorrow but just knowing He is with me is confidence enough. I truly love My God and savior. I know so much more now! He intervened again in my life!! I know most men in here pretend like they are content but being sure of Gods peace and purpose is something I pray they receive. Not only for these men but for anyone who is suffering.

    It is my prayer tonight that everyone knows their worth in the Kingdom of Heaven. Often it is the exact opposite of what the world says about us, and we should all be glad in that revelation. God's will and way is unsearchable and full of love. So, knowing God loves us is all we need to overcome. Wisdom in the fear or love of God is how I pray we all deal with the storm. Praise the God on High in the name of Jesus…Amen.

REVEALED IN THE PIT

<u>Seg. December 18, 2016 – Sunday Morning</u>

This morning I woke up thinking about my troubled son. See it's even hard to say troubled. My son is so special and called by God. He is easy to love but fails to love himself. He blames himself for mine and his mom's disobedience to the lord. Today I read that my disobedience not only affects me but also will have a direct effect on the people around me, including my children. What a responsibility!! It's a great revelation from the Lord today.

Although it's tough to acknowledge, it's just another reason to follow what God wants. No one can live in peace in disobedience to God. If we are obedient to His way, I am confident in life peaceful and full of love. I don't speak in terms of circumstances but in spirit.

I know my heart and its faithfulness will be tested by this life of seasons and circumstances. My God, I'm in solitary for the 7th day for absolutely nothing <u>but God's will</u>!! Put that hat on and wear it!!

Well, today I wear it and although it's difficult, I am happy to be alone with my God and His majesty. "For when I am weak, then I am strong". God truly shows His strength in the times we cannot…Amen

REVEALED IN THE PIT

<u>Seg. December 19, 2016 – Monday morning</u>

My 8th day on lockdown! I had the strangest dream this morning. I dreamt about my grandfather and my closest cousins. I know my grandfather is getting old, I hope he is ok today. As for me, I am really starting to feel the pressure of not only being on lockdown but also the holiday is right around the corner. I'm hoping God makes a way soon. I still haven't heard anything from anybody. My mom, of course, sent me a Christmas card. I love that woman so much. I want to be the best I can be for her. It upsets me, I worry her so often

This next year will be different. I know my God is faithful. His promises are true and full of glory. I know the things I must change, I intend to do so. I am really having a revival in the cage. God is showing me so much, I am worthy! Still, I'm struggling with my thoughts. But in this condition, I believe it is to be expected.

I've only been allowed to go outside once, and it was freezing and too cold to bare. Outside means standing in a kennel much like for a dog. I tried to enjoy the air but even that doesn't seem free anymore. I will not return to the segregation "yard" again! Just more suffering out there.

I long to hear the voice of my loved ones and children. I really miss my kids. I pray God keeps them safe and allows them to see me next year. I haven't seen them since I received this 32-year bid, earlier this year. How I'd love to visit with them!

This morning is another tough one, but God is with me. May He be with all the families who are not with all the ones they love this holiday. God bless them with his strength and love…Amen. "1 Peter 4:1-2, since Christ suffered for us in the flesh, arm yourselves also with the same mind, for he who has suffered in the flesh has ceased from sin, that he no longer should live the rest of his time in the flesh, for the lust of men, but for the will of God" – I'm surely suffering and am grieved terribly this scripture reminds me to endure it with the same mind Christ had during this trial. Success follows suffering with the mind of Christ! I will strive to maintain a godly attitude, as I suffer and know it's my attitude that glorifies God, not my suffering.

Louis Lopez

Seg. December 20, 2016 – Tuesday

This morning I woke up in tears. After breakfast I had a terrible dream. I seem to have a horrible spirit, either living with me or in me.

The dream I had was too disgusting to talk about. There is no reason or way that my dream came from God. This enemy hates the fact that I refuse to serve my flesh. This thing hates my need for the Lord. The faces and things I saw in my dream were horrific, the actions of it were even worse. My God and I will get to the bottom of this, so I can move forward in my life. I've never been so upset because of a dream. I honestly woke up crying and asking why? It's just about 8am and I am beside myself. I am so tired and am now afraid to go to sleep. What the heck?

I just want to give my all to God. I know I've been around bad spirits before. I know these spirits want me to kill myself. By the grace and power of God, I will not give in. I believe I saw my enemy this morning. Lust is his name and I rebuke it in the name of Jesus Christ.

Christ, please see my pain and willingness for your healing power over my life. I cannot face this adversary alone. Possess my body Lord with the <u>Holy Spirit</u>. Gee, now my pen wants to go out! Bring forth your light into my soul and cleanse me of these old thoughts and attitudes. Help me to be honest and uplifting to all that cross my path. Hold my enemy's captive and lose all strongholds that this wicked world has drawn to me. Please Father God, I beg of you to answer this prayer in the name of Jesus Christ…Amen

I just saw 3 or 4 men leave the hole this morning. I couldn't help but be disappointed. I feel like I'm not going to talk to anyone for the holidays. I don't understand this whole situation. I haven't tried to or made any attempts to hurt or do anything that would cause me to be here. I know I've made some wrong decisions, but none that would cause this! I'm not feeling well right now. I do not want to be defeated but this doesn't feel right.

I hope to hear something soon. No one has tried to let me know anything. This is the worst thing next to death. By now, I'm sure my family knows my situation and I'm sure they are worried, I've only been in seg. one time before. I did something to earn it though. This I just don't understand.

I know they can only hold me for up to 30 days. I'm hoping to hear from someone from the outside soon. I always hope the next day will be a better one. Regretfully, today so far is not as good as yesterday. Again, I feel dead inside, I feel like dying. I miss all my loved ones so much. I hope they don't think I've done anything crazy. I hope they aren't mad at me. I really want to talk to someone…I'm alone. I'm struggling, I am confused, I am low.

REVEALED IN THE PIT

Seg. December 20, 2016 – Tuesday afternoon

    I still am hurting pretty bad. Lockdown really has its way of playing on one's mind. I keep thinking about stuff that either isn't real or doesn't matter. It seems like every time I lay down to relax, my mind goes into overdrive. I hate my mind and I wish I wasn't against so much.

    I am strong though, I look at myself in the mirror and tell myself "to relax, and gods will shale be done!" Who does that? A guy in solitary confinement, that's who! ☺ Wow, a smile I guess that's a step in the right direction. Well, it is day 9, solitary confinement. I just would like some sign or hear from someone. A freaking officer would even be nice. I haven't really talked to anyone.

Mental health asks me if I'm ok every day and I just give them the thumbs up. Sure do want to be moved to the freakin rubber room. I am strong! I am able! UGH!!! A man like me is definitely not cut out for this type of treatment!! :{ I keep thinking about what I was doing last year. I got the opportunity to provide for Christmas. It was so nice to wake up with my babies after a night of wrapping presents with my love. Gosh, I miss them. I keep thinking about losing them. I know it's not up to me but still anyone could understand from where I sit. I think so deeply about everything, I hope God sees my heart in all of this. I hope He is hearing my prayers and holding me in my sufferings.

Dang, I hope I get mail today. I wish I had some envelopes! I used the one they gave me to write my love. I wonder if she's thinking or praying for me. I really wonder if she still loves me. Ok, that's enough of that nonsense. My mind again. I was reading the book of Isaiah, so I guess I'll get back to that. 2:30pm, not so full of the spirit (just the truth).

<u>Seg. December 20, 2016 – Tuesday evening</u>

So, not a bad ending to a bad day. It's around six and it's time to eat!! After my shower, I asked the C.O. if they knew why I was in here. They looked at my chart and said, "it's so vague we don't know". It is an investigation though, I also heard today, that this sometimes happens, and they usually get you out within 10 days.

So, once again, God has brought hope into my heart. He must be filled with laughter when He sees how ridiculous I am sometimes! What a Father! Well Father, I'm still trying to be the best son for Your Glory, liking/loving. I fail and die every day, but I never go too long without giving the God on High, my Father, his due. He has my heart and that will never change. Isaiah 49:15-16...Amen

Louis Lopez

<u>Seg. December 21, 2016 – Wednesday – Morning</u>

So, it's Wednesday, my 10th day of extreme suffering. I slept ok but woke up thinking about my children. It's been 8 months without seeing them, the longest was 9 months. So not quite there but it's super hard nonetheless. I'm hoping to see them on a regular basis as the New Year begins.

Last night I read the book of Lamentations, a book written by Jerimiah the Profit. The "weeping profit" writes almost a poem to God about fallen Israel. So many of the things he says were exactly out of my prayer book!! Repentance was the theme, without true repentance God cannot/will not forgive. I read one of the Psalms of David. He reported to the Lord about his indiscretions and sin of murder. I realized that it took him a year to really face what he'd done wrong in front of God.

Gosh, a whole year and some serious suffering (loss of his child) to come to full sorrow and repentance.

I wonder about my repentant life. I think about the things I still need deliverance from and the things God has truly forgiven of me. I obviously have some searching to do. I really believe this labor is connected to my unrepentant heart. It's so easy to be regretful for something, but not repentant. Repentance is deeper than just having regret. Repentance is from the whole heart which allows God to see your surrender and powerlessness in sin.

I ask the Father of all, to search me and find the strongholds that are causing me to fail, to find me forgiveness through repentance. I thank you Father for your patience and love for your son. I am not worthy to be healed by your forgiving hands; but because of the blood of the lamb, Jesus Christ, I am saved. Help me Father, to receive your truth and wisdom, to guide me to a repentance for the forgiveness of my sinful ways…Amen

REVEALED IN THE PIT

<u>Seg. December 21, 2016 – Wednesday afternoon</u>

I've been as usual, in deep thought about so many things. I've been thinking mostly about what it is I lie to myself about that leads me to things unforgiven. I really have a lot to face. The truths about my case, my relationship with my lady, my relationship with my mom and children, my current situation, and the list goes on, but those are the main things.

It seems this whole year I've been focusing on the things "I don't deserve" or the things "people don't do for me". I realize how sometimes I can be SOOO needy and fearful. It really comes down to pride and selfishness. Pride is so dangerous! It is a sin that is older than the world itself!

Often, I am humble and ready to sacrifice my wants for others. It makes me happy to know that something God has given me is really being able to see the service I offer despite myself. Thank you, Lord.

The danger comes when I feel like people don't treat me the way <u>I expect</u> all the time. Expectations and pride are separated by a thin line. It's easy to harp on how others are treating me. How others affect me, me, me!!! It's pride and not selflessness.

I am, by nature a protector. Being a protector cannot be done by my own reasoning or will. When I try that it always fails, and I end up the one who needs protecting. The devil is a liar. I am realizing that protection only comes from God and His security is without end. I can protect, still but only through the wisdom and guidance the Word provides.

So much easier said, especially from someone who's been severely abused and humiliated. Someone who for so long, couldn't protect himself. I have grown with the wrong thinking pattern that I can protect by my own will to make my inner self feel ok. I must realize that being Christ like is surrender and patience in waiting on the wisdom of the Lord. Control is not my business anymore!

Louis Lopez

<u>Seg. December 21, 2016 – Wednesday evening</u>

Tonight, I opened my bible to Phil 1:12-14, "I want you to know brethren that the things which actually happened to me have turned out for the furtherance of the gospel. So, that it has become evident to the whole palace guard, and to all the rest, that my chains are in Christ: and most of the brethren in the Lord, having become confident by my chains, are much bolder to speak the word without fear."

This is a pure indication of the bravery of Paul. It says to me that my imprisonment is being used to further the gospel. Acts 8:1-4 says my persecution can be productive. This scripture has spoken to me that joy is not a product of good circumstances, joy appears when we are wholly involved in trusting and serving God in any circumstances – good or bad! Paul shows this while writing to the church of Philippi from a Roman jail, chained to a Roman soldier! Attitude people, Attitude!!

In this day, just days away from Christmas, I think about the gifts that we receive. Those gifts, for the most part we use. I just read in the Word that the gifts God gives, we are with the same faith to use to bring His light into the world, no matter our circumstances. Tonight, has been a good night. God, through His Word, brings my wrong thinking to a stop.

God, through the Holy Spirit, and for His will, will "stop" or "put stops" in our way for His greater good. So many lessons from a good Father. Thank you, Father for your loving grace. No matter my circumstances, you are all I need to be joyful. Tonight, I smile, even in this pit, for the knowledge and hope I have in You. I love you. In the Name of Jesus, Amen.

Seg. December 22, 2016 – Thursday Morning

    Still in the SHU This morning I woke up early to pray for the men who have their disciplinary hearings today. I'm always drawn to recite Jesus prayer for His disciples and followers before He is crucified, John 17:6-26. I remember while I was fighting this case in the county jail, touching each prisoner's cell while they slept and moving the words of Jesus through the cell doors! Truly was amazing, even though most of the men were sleeping and never knew what I was doing, there was always one awake to say Thank you. It was Gods way of letting me know He was with me.

    Speaking of that, last night I received a letter from my friend and mother of my children! She is so great, I am so blessed to have her in my corner.

I can't express enough how just a few kind words can change my day. Although, yesterday wasn't a terrible one, she made it a blessing even more. I hope to hear from the love of my life next. I have children from both women and it's a grace we are one working family even in this. They will both be attending my mom's annual Christmas party this year, especially with what's happened. It will be tough for all, that's for sure. My prayer this morning is for them during these holidays and the ones ahead.

Lord, God of Heaven and Earth, Hear my prayer in the name of Jesus. Father, our loved ones are mourning the storm, during this year's Christmas season. I am crushed and chained, have mercy on us, Lord. Make it possible for the whole family to enjoy and celebrate the coming of your Son, Jesus. We need your wisdom, Lord, to understand and withstand this separation. Bring unity through love and forgiveness in my family as they come together to celebrate. Love them my God, as You have loved me. My children are yours, Father. My mom, dad, brothers and sisters are Yours, Father. My nieces and nephews are yours, Father. You are love and we love you and are thankful you are our God. Merry Christmas, Father. I offer you all that you've given me today as I have nothing in nothingness. Bring joy to all this year. In the Holy name of Jesus Christ, Amen.

Louis Lopez

REVEALED IN THE PIT

<u>Seg. December 22, 2016 – Thursday Afternoon</u>

I'm currently reading the book of Jeremiah. Wow, what a profit! I'm seeing a lot of myself in Jeremiah. He goes through a lot in the world and with God. His sufferings are crazy and make mine seem so mild. God really has had mercy on me.

Right now, I'm really sad and starting to realize this cell is where I will be celebrating Christmas. It will be a tough weekend for sure. I keep going over in my mind what I might have done wrong for this facility to put me out of population. I wonder if someone was making threats on my life. I wonder if someone is saying things about me that aren't true. I don't see how or why this has happened. I just see Gods will in all of it.

Like Jeremiah, it's hard to understand why God allows His children to endure such labors. I am locked away from all things during my favorite time of the year! This was such a tough year for me and my family. I just don't understand why it has to end like this. Right now, I am completely surrendered to God. He is my strength, seriously full of despair though. Can one be despaired and still have hope? I believe so.

I have hope that I will be closer to God through this time. I have hope that my family is relying on God and He is keeping them together with love. I hope they are all being kind to one another, especially during this stress filled time. It just doesn't seem right that we stress during such a wonderful time of year. I'm faithful, blessed, yet broken…

Jeremiah 17:14-18 – Prayer for deliverance, "Heal me O Lord, and I shall be healed; save me and I shall be saved, for you are my praise." Indeed, they say to me, where is the work of the Lord? Let it come now! As for me, I have not harried away from being a shepherd who follows you, nor have I deserved the woeful day. You know what comes out of my lips, it was right there before you. "Do not be a terror to me, you are my hope in the day of doom". Let them be ashamed who persecute me, but do not let me be dismayed. Bring on them, the day of doom, and destroy them with double destruction. Pretty powerful and how I feel and pray right now.

REVEALED IN THE PIT

<u>Seg. December 22, 2106 – Thursday evening</u>

Just was in deep thought about my mom. So much so that I'm pretty much in tears. I sometimes feel like such a burden to her. I can't understand how she could be proud of a son with so many problems. I know I shouldn't think like this but after 10 or 11 days of lockdown you start to wonder about your worth. I'm so glad I have my bible here with me.

Anyways, I want so much to make her happy. I know she blames herself for my failures in life. She has showed me more love than anyone on the planet. I've done things to hurt her to many times.

I don't want my pride to get in the way. I don't want to think about my failures as a son. Right now, though, I am forced to for some reason. She is probably thinking about me today. Well, Mom I'm thinking about you too. I'm sorry if I've put other things and people before you. I hope that in this lifetime I can make up for all the heartache I've caused you. I love you.

Tonight, has been full of ups and downs. My mind still thinks it's running things! I know getting my thoughts under control will take time to master. I go from life to death like quick, from hope to hopeless. God is really showing me a lot.

Although, I don't understand my circumstance, it's great to know I'm not alone. Let me say that again...I'm NOT ALONE! I hope they let me out tomorrow. If not, I know I'll be here for Christmas. Gosh that hurts! I hope the family is OK tonight. Life goes on for them while mine comes to a stop for now. I hope I can get a good night's rest...

Seg. December 23, 2016 – Friday morning

It's about 8:30am and I still don't know what's going on! Yesterday I heard some chatter that they might be moving me to another facility. I just asked the C.O. what was happening, and he said he'd look into it. I hope he lets me know something soon. It is one thing to know, it's another to not know, especially if I did nothing wrong.

I don't know why they would take me off this yard! I'm beginning to think it's a security issue. I think someone didn't like me and dropped a kite to have me removed! All anyone has to say is they are afraid for their life, even if they aren't. I just can't see who though or why? It would have to be somebody from my past. What a joke!

I really wish I could talk to my family! I'm sleeping less and less. Last night I literally had to talk myself to sleep. I had another crazy dream, mostly about me losing my family. I was like this drifter with this crew of others that just drifted around. One girl in my dream asked if I was truly alone. She asked if I wanted to be in their "drifting" crew. I remember telling her yes. When she asked if I had a family, I told her, "yes, once", but that it was gone and in the past. So, sad!!

Maybe that's my biggest fear, losing my family, with God, though, there is no fear. So, I believe it's the enemy throwing those "fiery darts" at me in my sleep. The sad truth is I don't feel like I have a family anymore. I've only talked to my kids a handful of times over the past two months or so. I feel like I'm being kicked out of their lives. It's not fair!

Geez, I thought the Thanksgiving holiday was hard! I'm so tired! I am going to lay down and wait with patience to see what's going to happen here. I saw they already let one guy out, so maybe me next!

December 23, 2016 – Friday afternoon – Still Seg.

Well, it's afternoon now and still no word, looks like I get to spend this Christmas in the box (no pun intended!!) I actually took a nap this morning. I cried myself to sleep. I feel like God is asking me to let go of the outside world. Maybe just for this time? Well, obviously He doesn't want me around for much at all.

I had such a great time with the kids and family last year. I knew it might be my last for a long time, so I wanted to make it count. Now that my worst nightmare has manifested, I can honestly say last year doesn't matter. This pain cuts deep. Maybe they'll let me call this weekend? I don't know though, because a call from me might make it worse for everyone. I feel like letting them forget about me or at least not think about me to help ease their pain. I don't even have the power to do such things. I'm suffering...

This is truly a tough price to pay after all that's happened this year. For it to end like this just doesn't feel like my God. It feels like He hates me. Day's like this I feel cursed. He has let all wrath come upon me. I really didn't do anything to deserve this suffering. I know my mind wasn't always where it needed to be but, I never stopped loving the Lord. I recognized Him through it all only for it to end up like this.

I know it wouldn't be so hard if it wasn't during the holiday's I know my kids will think I hate them for not even calling. The little ones are going to blame themselves! Maybe even the older ones! My heart is crushed, every day that passes I feel like a piece of me is dying. Why would God want this for anyone? I certainly didn't. Have I been so wicked? Am I not facing the truth that I belong in prison? Am I lying to myself thinking God still is for me?

It feels like He walked away from me! Am I wasting my time with faithful prayer when He just rejects them? Am I His vomit? Is He regretful of the day He made me? Have I brought curse, to my family and children? Is that why I'm condemned?

Why am I alive? What does my life mean? Is there no good in me that God sees? Am I not His child? I'M SICK. Merry Christmas to me, what a joke...

Pacing back and forth, back and forth. I can't even pick up my bible today. I don't think I'm going to stay at this facility. I have no write-up, so I am going to be moving. I know the facility has 30 days to place me. So, two more weeks or so. I don't know where I'm going to start the New Year. I wish they would just keep me in this box until it kills me. I don't even want to meet anyone else. I don't trust anyone at this point.

Louis Lopez

Seg. December 24, 2016 – Saturday morning

It's Christmas Eve! Last night was a sleepless one. I don't recall another time in my life I've felt more alone. I have no emotion right now. I'm numb, I can see the smiles and hear the laughter of all the ones I love. They fade away and the coldness of this cell reminds me of all I've become; a prisoner.

I can barely write. My hands are shaking and unsteady. All I want to do is sleep through these holidays. Every time I try to close my eyes, they are quickly opened as if some other entity forces them. I am grieved today for sure. I won't be broken as in my heart I'm crying out to the Lord! Amen

I know Satan can't curse what God has blessed. Still it's almost impossible right now to not let

him contain me. Does that even make sense?
Gosh am I losing it? Will I find victory or death?
Help me God – Tears!

December 25, 2016 – Christmas Day (Sunday morning)

Yesterday I could barely breathe, last night I prayed for rest and He gave it to me. Halleluiah! This morning I prayed to be revealed Gods presence in this place of suffering. He spoke to me! He spoke to me!!

Philippians 1:12-14 says, "But I want you to know, brethren, that the things which happened to me have actually turned out the furtherance of the gospel, (13) – so that it has become evident to the whole palace guard, and to all the rest, that my chains are in Christ's; (14) - and most of the brethren in the Lord, having become confident by my chains, are much more bold to speak the word without fear".

The words from the Lord through Paul while in a Roman prison. I know my duty is to further the truth about righteousness and redemption. I don't know what's ahead, but I know I will be fighting to reach broken people. Although my heart is completely broken at the moment. I am finding comfort in having a purpose on this Earth.

For the rest of this year I'm going to focus on the things I have and try not to focus on the things I don't. It will be a task as I am without much on this Christmas Day. I'm done writing until next year as my strength is low. Still suffering!!

Seg. January 1, 2017 – New Year's Day – Sunday morning

Haven't entered anything in a week. Been silencing my heart in this struggle. Since I've endured a cold Christmas and New Year. During this past week I was given the opportunity to call my family. I also received letters from all the people I love. God answered all my prayers. Well most, still in this cage. Hopefully this week!

Truly this was Gods will, the other night I was on the phone with the love of my life. She asked why I sounded so happy. Obviously, my answer was because I finally got to her the voice I so longed to hear. Although that was true, I also believe it was because I was filled with the Holy Spirit.

I've cried almost every day, this has been a tough test of faith. Still I remain and have been kept strong by Gods will and hand. I read the entire book of Revelation. Such a blessing and eye opener.

My lady told me that lately she'd been really depressed. I wanted so bad to tell her about what God promises us in eternity. We must suffer and be tempted in this fallen world. If we persevere with faith and patience, Gods reward is bliss. I can't wait to really spend some time to explain to all I love what God has revealed to me.

Honestly, I am blessed today to be totally alone with my Lord and Savior. I appreciate so much more now that He's stripped me down and brought me low. He has prepared me for the fight I have before me. Today I remain in chains and suffering but am faithful in the unseen reasons. 2 Corinthians 4:16-18 "Therefore we do not lose heart, even though our outward man is perishing, yet the inward man is being renewed day by day. (17) For our light affliction, which is but for a moment, is working for us a far more exceeding and eternal weight of glory. (18) While we do not look at the things which are seen. For the things which are seen are temporary, but the things which are not seen are eternal". Amen

Seg. January 2, 2017 – Monday morning

Just woke up! Looks like no movement today. Seems like I've been in here for a lifetime! I'm always hoping on tomorrow, Day 22. 24-hour lockdown is no joke.

I'm feeling alone again. My mind is full of thoughts about everything. Last night I went to sleep thinking about my case and my time. It is truly difficult to think of what could become of my life, if I don't get relief through my appeal, I can't even think of that. God gives me His promise and I just live waiting for them to manifest.

Still feeling down this morning, I miss everyone so much. I miss my love. Remembering her in my arms always makes me feel better. She believes I'm coming home soon. I think we are in doubt about our union because we haven't taken the final step of our relationship…marriage. I really don't see myself marrying anyone else. She means that much to me. OK, this is going to things beyond my control and to a place I don't want to be. I guess I'll lay down, get into the Word and take some deep breaths. Mornings are the hardest, when you're totally without.

Seg. January 2, 2017 – Monday afternoon

Read a little from 2 Corinthians and the book of Galatians. Couldn't fall asleep, so here I am. The more I lay here, the more my mind goes to work. I keep wondering about where I'll end up. I'm thinking about putting in for that mentoring program in Denver. It would be nice to give back and be close to my family. Hopefully this circumstance doesn't affect my security status.

I really wish I knew what happened here. Guess I'll know soon enough! I really want to use the phone. I'm going to be on it for a whole day when I get out of here. Can't wait to hear my oldest daughter talk about her teenage life. I'm sure she's worried about her dad. She is so grown up and definitely headed for a successful life. All my children are special, and I hope they never suffer the way I am. My prayer is for their mothers and them.

May God have mercy on them and provide wisdom, so they can make good decisions toward their destiny. My God is worthy and breaks all yokes and generational curses. Through the name of Jesus Christ. I pray my suffering imprisoned leads to a testimony to further the gospel, not only for my children but to all who are called to the work of the cross. Amen.

REVEALED IN THE PIT

<u>Seg. January 2, 2017 – Monday evening</u>

Well it's almost the end of another day in the box. Hopefully coming to the end of my stay. I'm trying as hard as I can to keep myself busy. It's starting to get impossible. I've been pushing up the floor as much as I can. With only 3 small meals, it's hard to find the strength.

Louis Lopez

Seg. January 2, 2017 – Monday night

It's about 10 pm and I again cannot get to sleep, so I read first John tonight and realized so much about love. I thought, "Who in my life has sacrificed more than God?" No one has shown me more love through sacrifice than the Almighty. I truly do owe Him my life.

I've been struggling with worthlessness lately. I have tried to fight my thoughts because I know worthlessness is not of God. Today I realize I lack discipline. So as I practice better thoughts, my mind opens to so many good things. And with good things in my thoughts my heart is filled with love, Filled with Christ.

REVEALED IN THE PIT

Seg. January 3, 2017 – Tuesday morning

Still here! It's around 9:30am and all moves have been made. Looks like I'm stuck for yet another day. Mornings are so tough, oh well, Gods will and not mine!!!

Twenty-three days! Starting to come unglued a little. I've seen so many men leave, it messes with my mind. Last night I tossed and turned until Twelve or so. I'm still faithful but feeling weak.

Enduring this, I'm confident and will prove me faithful. I'm sure one day soon, I will be fully prepared to teach love and truth with the confidence it requires. Speak it and live it! Now, to remember how to talk to people again…LOL!

I must've sounded crazy on the phone the other night! If they only had an idea of how grave my circumstance, I pray they never do. Sadly, my family go through their own suffering and tests of faith. I know they all root for me, as I do for them.

I miss them so much, I'll never take their love for granted ever again. It makes me so mad when I think about how I've been so selfish – (not condemned, just convicted) I love you guys!!!

REVEALED IN THE PIT

Seg. January 3, 2017 – Tuesday evening

Son hear my voice, I know you're suffering, and I want you to understand some things about me, and your condition. First, I want you to know I love you more than you can ever fathom. You are my favorite son. I hate it, you are hurting the way you are. I want you to know, son, this was not my will for your life, it still isn't. This was your will! I only wanted good things and victory for your life, I still do.

I was standing in your way and warned you so many times. Because you didn't heed my warnings, son, you are now experiencing the only thing you can…loss. I brought you to this place for this moment. You are finding repentance here with me now. Thank you, son, I forgive you, I never stopped

Now, I need you to see your worth in my kingdom. You can only rest in my peace when you see your uniqueness as a virtue. I've given you all you need, all the talents and gifts to find the path of redemption.

You've used all I've given you as an investment in corruption. I command you now, son, to use your gifts for my righteous work. I am faithful you can and will. Before you are able though son you need to transform your heart from pain, anger, regret and worthlessness. I am Love, be filled with me and prove worthy. You must be transformed from within, son, then and only then can you live in the circle of righteousness.

Living inside the circle of righteousness, through love will give you the power you need for the destiny I've set before you. Isn't that what you want? You can only find your true identity and purpose in me and through me.

Once you find and step into the circle, you will face any opposition without anxiousness or fear. It is my promise son, in the circle of righteousness you will more than overcome. You will with confidence and authority be able to withstand any man, circumstance or opposition that comes against you, my son.

Remember son, before you face anything, you must proclaim my name and its righteousness. Be a warning to all evil that you are covered in the blood of my son Jesus, choose me son, choose a life of love and righteousness and be redeemed!

2 Corinthians 8: 10-12 says, "And in this I give advice: it is to your advantage not only to be doing what you began and desiring to do a year ago; but now you also must complete the doing of it that as there was a readiness to desire it, so there also may be a completion out of what you have. For if there is first a willing mind, it is accepted according to what one has and not according to what he does not have."

Revelation from the Lord Almighty!

AMEN

January 4, 2014 – Wednesday

RELEASED

REVEALED IN THE PIT

www.ingramcontent.com/pod-product-compliance
Lightning Source LLC
Chambersburg PA
CBHW052203110526
44591CB00012B/2066